PAC-MANIA!

BITING HUMOR
BY HALLER SCHWARZ

PINNACLE BOOKS   NEW YORK

ABOUT HALLER SCHWARZ

Haller Schwarz is Dick Chodkowski, Dan Dixon, Clem Scharwath and Rich Teich in Los Angeles. Plus Charlie Greene in Dusseldorf. Also Tony Haller. And Hank Schwarz.

This book is dedicated to the Heisenberg Principle of Uncertainty and Rich Teich's Mother.

No dedication would be complete, of course, without thanking Various Friends.

PAC-MANIA
Text Copyright © 1982 by Haller Schwarz
Illustrations Copyright © 1982 by Bally Midway Manufacturing Company

An original Pinnacle Books edition, published for the first time anywhere.

First printing, June 1982

I S B N : 0 - 5 2 3 - 4 1 9 2 5 - 2

Printed in the United States of America

PINNACLE BOOKS, INC.
1430 Broadway
New York, New York 10018

PAC-MAN OF THE YEAR.

PAC -O-LANTERN.

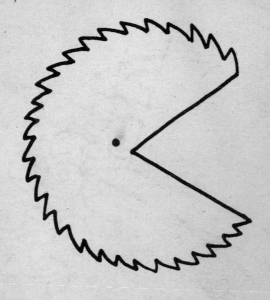

PAC-SAW.

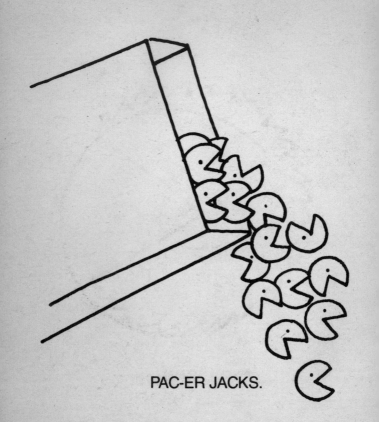

PAC-ER JACKS.

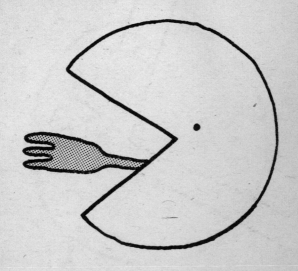

PAC-MAN WITH A FROG
IN HIS THROAT.

PAC-MAN SWALLOWING A LEMON.

PAC-STROKE.

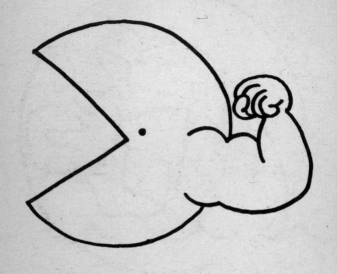

PAC LALANNE.

PACTERIA.

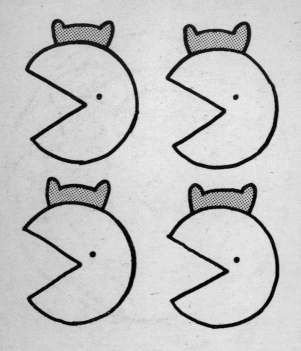

BOY SCOUT PAC.

PAC-MAN EATING CROW.

PAC-POCKET.

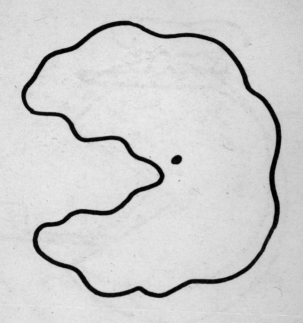

SOFT PAC.

GENERAL PACARTHUR.

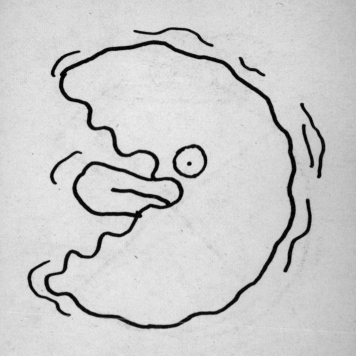

PSYCHO-PAC.

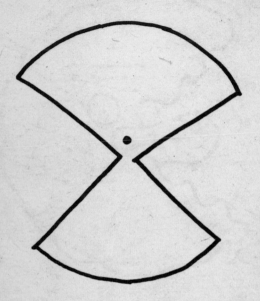

OVERACHIEVING PAC-MAN.

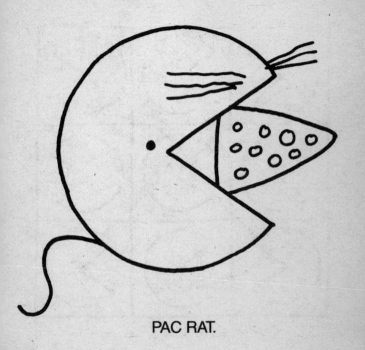

PAC RAT.

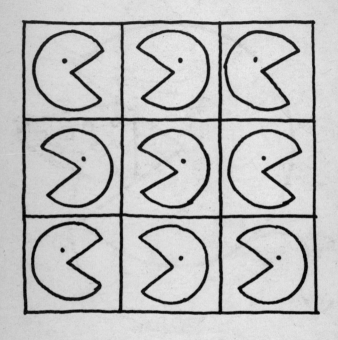

PAC-MEN ON HOLLYWOOD SQUARES.

OLD PACDONALD.

PAC-MAIL PHOTO.

LOVESICK PAC-MAN EATING
HIS HEART OUT.

GIFT PAC.

PAC-IN-THE-BOX.

PAC'S PEAK.

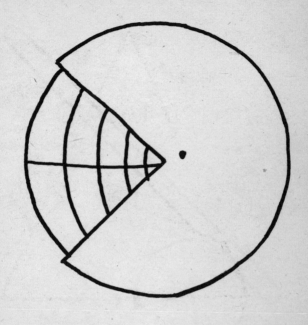

PAC-MAN WITH NEW DENTURES.

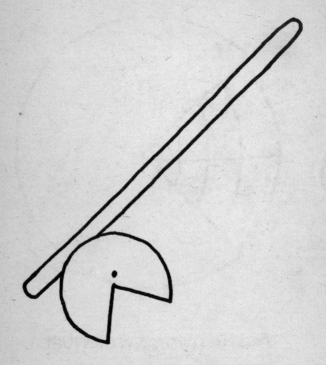

PAC-SCRATCHER.

SIX-PAC.

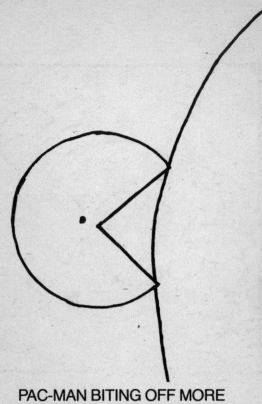

PAC-MAN BITING OFF MORE
THAN HE CAN CHEW.

PAC-MAN WITH BAD BREATH.

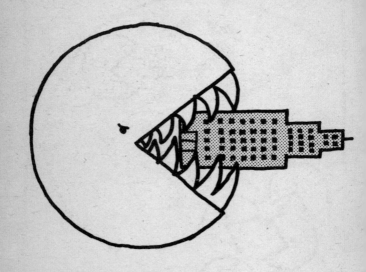

PACZILLA.

PAC-MAN WITH A BAD OVERBITE.

HYPER-EXTENDED PAC-MAN.

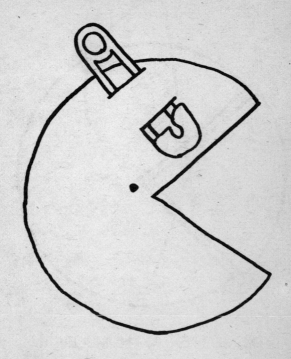

PUNK PAC.

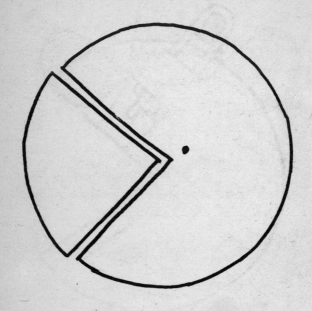

PAC-MAN EATING HUMBLE PIE.

PAC IN THE SADDLE AGAIN.

PACKERAL.

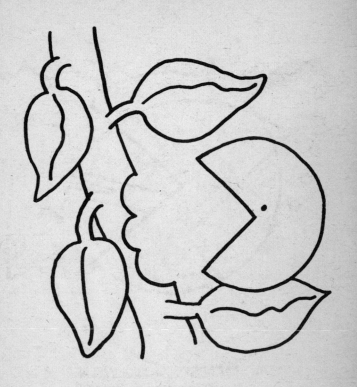

PAC AND THE BEANSTALK.

PAC-MAN SPEAKING WITH
FORKED TONGUE.

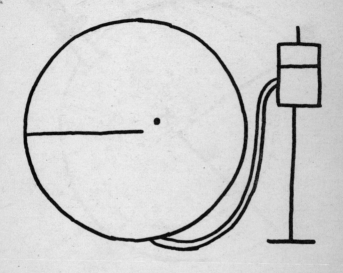

PAC-MAN BEING FED INTRAVENOUSLY.

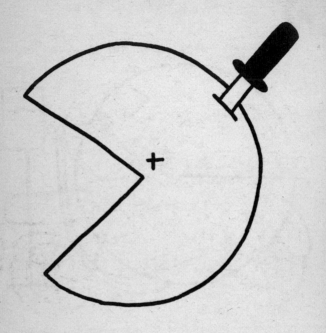

STABBED IN THE PAC.

LEADER OF THE PAC.

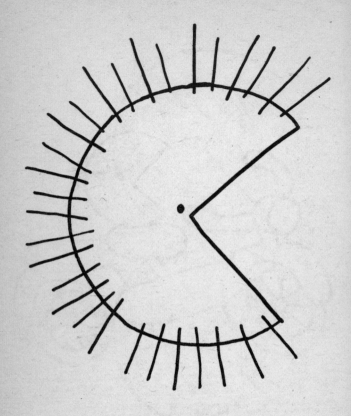

PACUPINE.

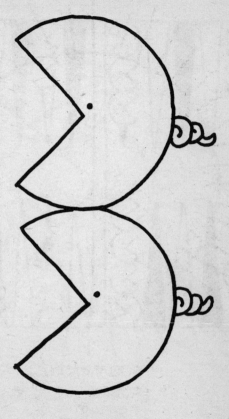

PIGGY-PAC.

PACGAMMON.

THAT OLD PAC MAGIC.

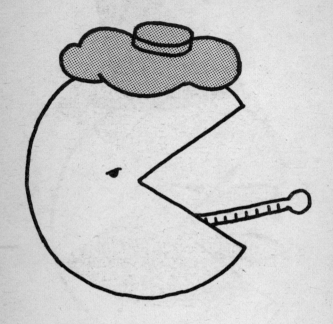

PAC-ACHE.

HOCKEY PAC.

PAC-MAN AND ROBIN.

THE PACSON FIVE.

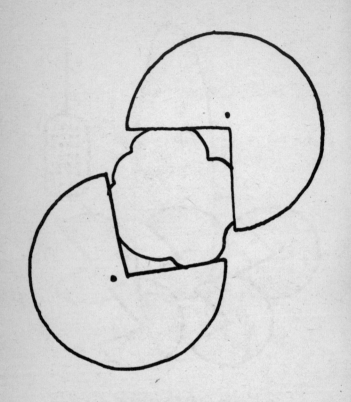

**PAC-MAN SITTING AROUND
CHEWING THE FAT.**

PAC-MAN ON A HUNGER STRIKE.

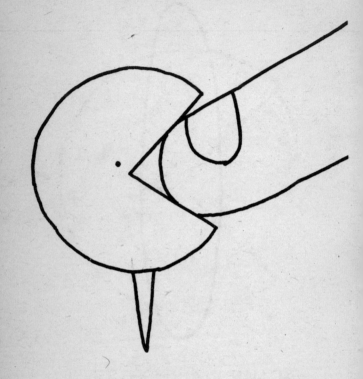

THUMB-PAC.

COUNT PACULA.

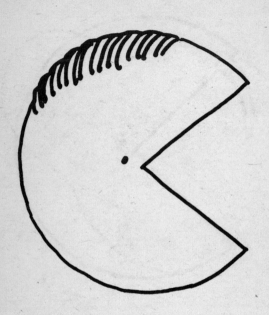

PAC-MAN WEARING A TOUPEE.

THE HUNCHPAC OF NOTRE DAME.

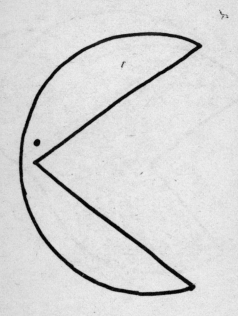

PAC-MAN'S MOTHER-IN-LAW.

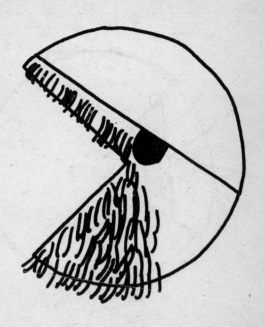

PACBEARD THE PIRATE.

PAC-MAN EATING A TV DINNER.

PAC-MAN WITH A TOOTHACHE.

PAC-MAN CHEWING TOBACCO.

PAC-MAN HAVING A FRIEND OVER
FOR DINNER.

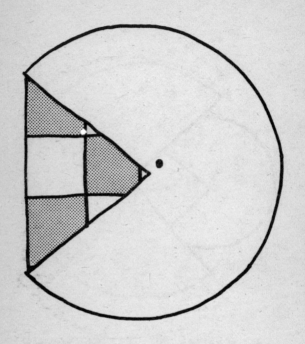

PAC-MAN SOLVING
THE RUBIK'S CUBE.

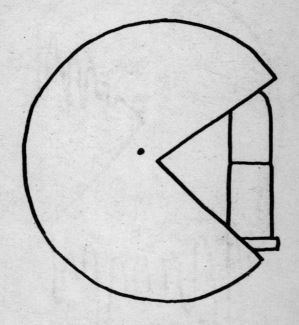

PAC-MAN BITING THE BULLET.

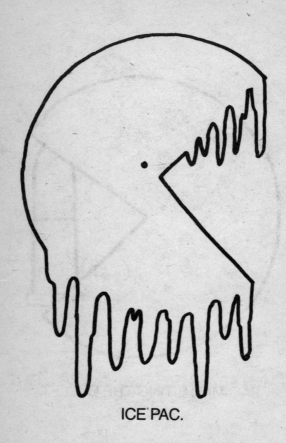

ICE PAC.

PAC-MAN AFTER GETTING CHEWED OUT
BY HIS BOSS.

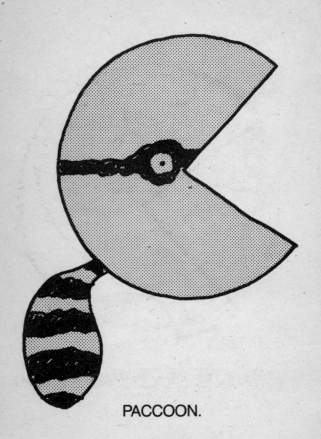

PACCOON.

PAC-MAN DRIVER'S LICENSE PHOTO.

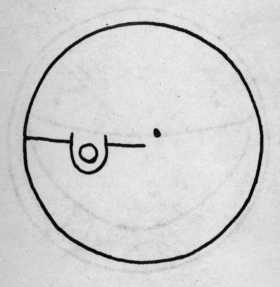

PAC-MAN KEEPING
LIP BUTTONED.

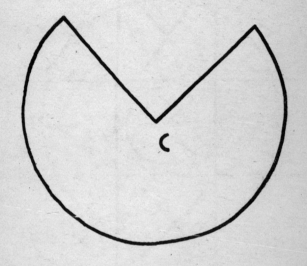

SLEEPING PAC-MAN.

TIC PAC TOE.

PAC-MOTHER SWALLOWING
HER PRIDE.

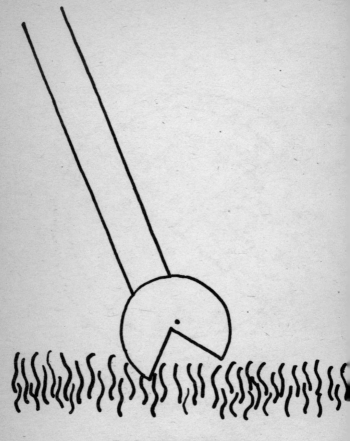

PACUUM CLEANER.

COMPAC CAR.

PACASSO.

PAC-ROAST AND
MASHED POTATOES.

PAC-MAN FINANCES.

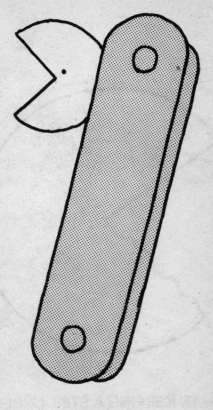

PAC-KNIFE.

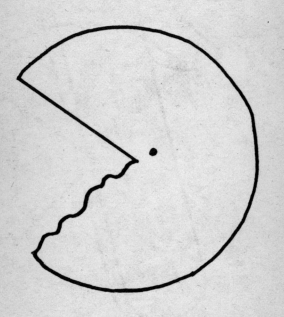

PAC-MAN KEEPING A STIFF UP-PER LIP.

PAC-DOG.

PAC-MAN DRESSED UP FOR
"LET'S MAKE A DEAL."

BIG PAC.

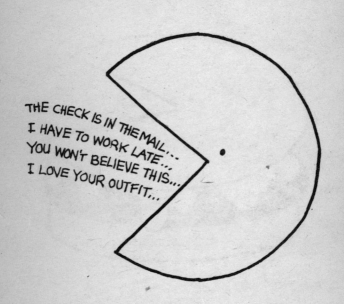

PAC OF LIES.

PAC-MAN OUT TO
LUNCH.

PAC-MAN FINISHING A KING
FIT FOR A MEAL.

PACARONI.

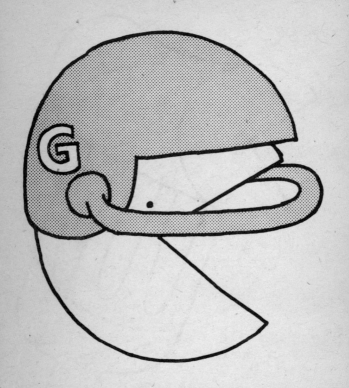

GREEN BAY PAC-ER.

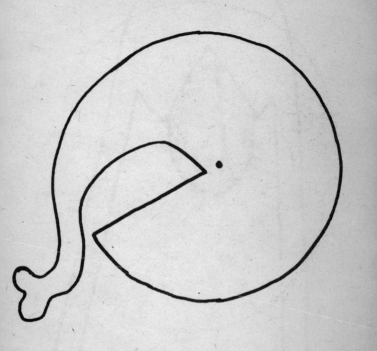

PACADERM.

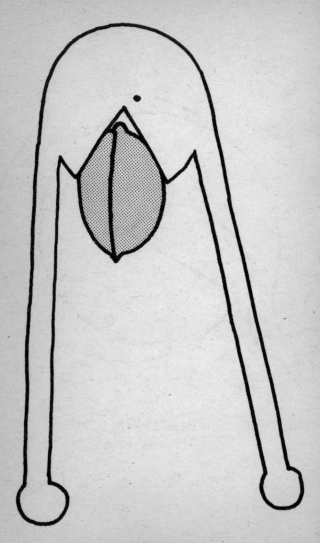

NUTPAC-ER.

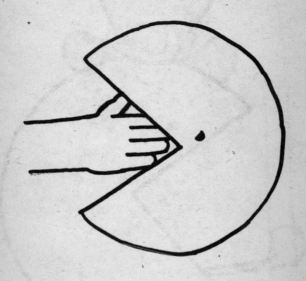

PAC-MAN BITING THE HAND
THAT FEEDS HIM.

ST. PAC-TRICK.

PAC-TICAL JOKE.

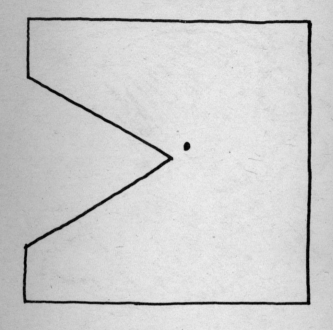

PREHISTORIC PAC-MAN.

SNOW PAC.

PAC TO THE DRAWING BOARD.